I0846009

Financial Literacy

The Foundation for Independence and Security

Table of Contents

Chapter 1. Introduction

Special Report: Financial Literacy - The Foundation for Independence and Security

In an increasingly complex financial landscape, ensuring one's independence and security can often seem a herculean task. Thankfully, the road to financial vigor may be much simpler than you think, even inviting. This Special Report titled, "Financial Literacy: The Foundation for Independence and Security", is designed to enlighten, empower, and embolden you to take the reins of your financial future. This comprehensive guide will make the seemingly intricate world of finance accessible and engaging, offering a vital exploration of topics such as budgeting, saving, investing, and debt management. It's time to remove the shroud of intimidation around financial literacy. This Special Report serves as a stepping stone towards mastering the financial realm, fostering the confidence needed to build towards economic independence and security. A financially literate you is just a few pages away! This isn't just a one-time purchase, it's an investment in your path to financial freedom. Time to turn the page and cast off the financial indecisiveness once and for all. Let's begin this journey together!

Chapter 2. Understanding the Basics of Financial Literacy

Financial literacy is your key to understanding how to save, invest, and make your money work for you. It's about the fundamental understanding of how money works, how to manage it, save it, invest it, and use it effectively. To demystify these basic concepts, let's take stock of what this entails.

2.1. The Fundamental Principles of Personal Finance

Personal finance encompasses all the decisions a person might make in managing their money - the act of budgeting, saving, investing, spending, and forecasting future financial trends. Let's take a glance at some of the cardinal rules that lay the foundation for sound personal finance:

1. **Live below your means**: The simplest yet most effective principle. Irrespective of how much you earn, always spend less. This creates a surplus, which can then be directed towards saving and investing.

2. **Invest early and often**: Due to the power of compound interest, a little money invested today could be worth more than a lot of money invested later. Make regular investments a part of your financial strategy.

3. **Never take on unnecessary financial risk**: Never risk more than you can afford to lose, especially when if you're nearing retirement. The potential for higher rewards usually comes with increased risk.

4. **Diversify**: Spreading your investments across a wide range of different types of assets and geographic areas can help lessen

risk. This strategy is designed to help you avoid "having all your eggs in one basket."

5. **The only thing certain about the stock market is its uncertainty**: While the stock market can be a good place to grow your wealth, it is also highly volatile. Always do thorough research and consider seeking advice from a financial advisor.

2.2. The Concept of Budgeting

Budgeting is the process of creating a plan for your spending. The principle revolves around organizing your income and expenses. Here's a step-by-step guide on how to establish your budget:

1. **Know your income**: Record your total income you get from your job and any additional sources.

2. **Identify your expenses**: Make a list of all your monthly expenses, both mandatory and discretionary.

3. **Subtract expenses from income**: Take your total expenses away from your total income. A positive balance indicates a surplus, while a negative balance signals a deficit.

4. **Make adjustments**: If you're showing a deficit, you will have to decrease your spending. If you have a surplus, you have additional money to put towards savings or investing.

5. **Stick to your budget**: The most crucial and often the hardest step. It requires discipline and commitment.

2.3. The Importance of Saving

Having a savings account allows you to cover unexpected costs without having to borrow money. For building an ample saving, consider: 1. **Emergency fund**: Aim to save at least three to six months' worth of living expenses. 2. **Set goals**: Having clear, defined goals can motivate you to save more and faster. 3. **Regular**

contributions: Even if it's a small amount, regular saving will add up over time.

2.4. Understanding Debt

While debt such as loans for education or a home can be useful for long-term wealth creation, excessive or unmanaged debt can create financial instability. Consider: 1. **Pay off high interest rate debts first**: This will save you money over the long run. 2. **Don't borrow for every purchase**: Save for large purchases instead of putting them on credit. 3. **Maintain a good credit score**: This can lower your borrowing costs in the future.

2.5. Investing Basics

Investment is the process of putting your money to work for you, creating wealth over time. Key points to remember when starting to invest are: 1. **Understand risk tolerance**: Higher risk investments have the promise of higher returns but also increased potential for loss. 2. **Explore various investment vehicles**: Consider stocks, bonds, mutual funds, real estate, among others. 3. **Invest for long-term**: Long-term investing can smooth out the highs and lows of the market.

In conclusion, understanding the basics of financial literacy is about creating a plan for achieving financial goals, being equipped to make informed financial moves, and ensuring that you are well-prepared for what the future may hold financially. Although mastering these basic principles may seem like a daunting task, remember that financial literacy is not a destination but a journey. Commit to lifelong learning, and the road to financial independence and security will unfold before you.

Chapter 3. The Importance of Budgeting

In order to build a robust financial life, it's crucial to relay the first cornerstone, budgeting. This essential tool supports financial management and ensures your resources are allocated in accordance to your priorities and goals, promoting an efficient and accountable utilization of finances.

3.1. Understanding Budgeting

At its core, budgeting is a process of creating a plan to spend your money. It's a blueprint for your financial life, outlining your income sources, your expenses, both recurring and occasional, and your savings and investment allocations. It aids in pinpointing areas of excessive spending, recognizing opportunities for savings, preparing for emergencies, and paving the way towards achieving financial objectives. Notably, budgeting is not just an exercise for those struggling financially—it's a powerful tool required irrespective of income brackets.

One of the consistent failures in budgeting is the perception that it's a restrictive mechanism, a leash to lead a miserly lifestyle. However, contrary to this belief, a budget is not there to limit your freedom, but to extend it. By being aware of where your money goes, a budget empowers you to take control of your financial destiny – to decide whether you want to continue spending your money on certain things or change your financial behavior.

3.2. The Benefits of Budgeting

Managing your financial resources effectively brings about various benefits.

1. **Financial Awareness** – By tracking income and expenses, budgeting increases your awareness regarding money matters. This ensures you are not oblivious to where your money comes from and how it's being spent.

2. **Controls Overspending** – Budgeting helps to keep your spending in line with your income, preventing fall into debt or living paycheck to paycheck.

3. **Helps in Achieving Goals** – A budget assists in planning and setting aside funds for long-term goals, such as buying a house, starting a business, or retirement planning.

4. **Emergency Preparedness** – A prudent budget factors in unexpected expenses or financial emergencies that life could throw your way. It helps cultivate a culture of saving and maintaining an emergency fund.

3.3. The Components of a Budget

An effective budget features several key components, including:

1. **Income**: This is the total money you have coming in, from wages, bonuses, investments, etc.

2. **Expenses**: These are your ongoing outlays. There are two main types—fixed and variable. Fixed costs are the same each month, such as rent or mortgage, insurance, or car payments. Variable costs fluctuate, like groceries, entertainment, or clothing.

3. **Savings**: This is money set aside for future use, including short term goals or emergency funds.

4. **Debt**: Any outstanding loans or credit card bills you need to repay.

To start crafting your budget, you have to initially gather detailed information on each of these elements.

3.4. Types of Budgeting Methods

There are several budgeting methods available, each with its unique approach. Here are a few:

1. **50/30/20 Rule:** This simple rule proposes allocating 50% of your after-tax income to needs, 30% to wants, and 20% to savings and debt repayments.

2. **Zero-Based Budgeting:** Every dollar of income is allocated to a category (needs, wants, savings, or debt repayment). The goal is that income minus expenses equals zero by the end of the month.

3. **Envelope Method:** This involves dividing your income into envelopes for different categories. Once an envelope is empty, spending for that category stops until the next budget cycle.

Adopt the approach that aligns most conveniently with your lifestyle, income, and financial goals.

3.5. Creating a Personal Budget

Constructing a personal budget involves several steps:

1. Identify your income: Gather all your income sources. Be sure to use your net income - the amount you take home after taxes, other deductions, or contributions.

2. Track and categorize your spending: Begin to list your expenses. Ensure to capture every penny spent. Categorize these expenses as wants or needs.

3. Set your goals: Decide on short-term (less than a year), mid-term (1-5 years), and long-term (5+ years) financial goals. It could be an exotic vocation, a new car, or your child's college fund.

4. Create your budget: Utilize information from the above steps to establish your budget. Remember the idea is income minus

outgo(valued goals + expenses) equals zero.

5. Stick to your plan: The most challenging step is sticking to your plan, but with constant practice, it becomes a habit. Make adjustments where necessary.

By acknowledging the importance of budgeting and using it as a tool to handle your finances effectively, you stand a solid chance of reaching your financial objectives. The power to achieve financial freedom is within your reach - one budget at a time. Starting today, free the chains of financial uncertainty, and embrace the path towards your financial goals.

Chapter 4. Transforming Saving into an Habit

Saving money consistently may sometimes seem like a daunting task, especially when immediate gratifying expenditures tug at our whims. But with discipline, determination, and understanding, we can transform saving from a chore into a habit. In this chapter, we'll deep-dive into the various aspects of saving as we guide you on the path to making it a lasting habit.

4.1. The Psychology of Saving

Firstly, it's important to recognize the psychological components driving our spending habits. We live in a consumer-focused society where we're constantly encouraged to buy and spend more. These social forces, coupled with our natural inclination towards immediacy and comfort, often push us towards short-term gratification at the expense of long-term financial health.

Understanding the psychological factors influencing our behaviour lets us create strategies to counteract them. For instance, linking saving with positive emotions, and visualizing the comfort and security of having savings, can be powerful motivators.

4.2. The Power of Goals

The first step in making saving a habit starts with establishing clear, actionable goals. Goals serve as a tangible marker for our progress, providing both motivation and direction. Start by identifying long-term goals, such as retirement savings, buying a home, or starting a business. Then, break these down into smaller, achievable short-term goals that lead up to the long-term goals over time.

For instance, if your long-term goal is to save €50,000 for a home deposit, break that into smaller, manageable savings targets of €1,000 each month. Keep track of your progress regularly to maintain motivation.

4.3. Creating a Savings Plan

A well-structured savings plan is integral to transforming saving into a habit. By planning, you're taking control of your money and deciding where it should go rather than wondering where it went.

Your savings plan should include the following components:

1. Income: Record all sources of income.

2. Expenses: Record all regular and occasional spending.

3. Savings goal: Record the amount you plan to save each month. Remember to align this with your set goals.

It's recommended to follow the 50/30/20 rule of thumb for budgeting. This rule proposes that you allocate 50% of your income to needs, 30% to wants, and the remaining 20% to savings and paying off debt.

4.4. Tools to Help You Save

In the age of technology, there are numerous tools to facilitate and automate the saving process.

1. Automatic transfers: Set up automatic transfers from your checking account to your savings account to ensure regular savings.

2. Mobile apps: Utilize savings and budgeting applications to track spending and savings.

3. Savings calculators: These tools can help you measure your savings progress toward your goals.

4.5. The Habit Loop

Making saving a habit means making it part of your routine. The 'Habit Loop' theory describes habits as a three-part process: . Cue: The trigger that initiates behaviour. . Routine: The behaviour itself. . Reward: The benefit gained from doing the behaviour.

In the case of saving, the cue could be receiving your monthly paycheck, the routine is the act of transferring a specific amount into your savings account, and the reward is seeing your savings grow, bringing you closer to your goals. By correlating the act of saving with positive reinforcement (reward), we rewire our brain to view saving as a beneficial and necessary act, thus forming a habit.

4.6. Overcoming Challenges

Despite best intentions, you may encounter obstacles in your savings journey. You might have unexpected expenses, or you may lose motivation. During these times, it's important to remain resilient and dedicated. Adjust your plan if necessary, but stay committed to the act of saving itself.

In summary, transforming saving into a habit involves educating ourselves, setting clear goals, making a savings plan, utilising available tools, understanding the habit formation process, and staying resilient in the face of challenges. Keep in mind that everyone's financial journey is personal, and there are no 'one-size-fits-all' methods. The most important ingredient in developing this habit is you – your dedication, commitment, and attitude towards saving.

Chapter 5. Investment: The Path Toward Wealth

Investing is one of the fundamental building blocks of economic security. Defined as the act of committing money or capital in order to gain profitable returns, as interest, income, or appreciation in value, investing serves as the most reliable path to growing wealth over the long run. Yet for many, it remains a misunderstood or even daunting concept.

5.1. Understanding Investments

Before you jump into the world of investments, it's critical to ensure you have a solid understanding of the basic principles. An investment could be buying property aiming for rental income and/or price appreciation, starting or buying into a business, or purchasing a financial product like a stock or bond. Each of these types of investments come with their own level of risk and reward, and understanding them is key to making smart investing decisions.

The primary reason someone invests their money is to earn a return on the amount invested. The return can come in two main forms: income and capital growth. Income refers to the regular payments you receive, such as rent, interest or dividends. Capital growth, or capital gain, is the increase in the value of your investment over time.

5.2. Managing Risk and Return

When you invest, you need to be aware of the potential risks and returns. It's important to remember that the returns from investments are typically proportional to the risk involved; the higher the chance of making money, the higher the risk of losing money. Therefore, consider your tolerance for risk and the time period over which you're planning to invest. This is known as your investment 'horizon'.

The concept of risk and reward is a fundamental one in the world of investing, and it can affect your potential for financial growth. Risk is the chance that the actual return on an investment will be different than the expected return. It comes in many forms, from credit risk (the chance that a borrower will not repay a loan) to market risk (the chance that an investment's value will decrease due to economic changes).

Conversely, the return on your investment is the money that you earn from the growth of your investment, as well as any income received from it, such as interest or dividend payments.

5.3. The Power of Compounding

One of the most powerful factors in investing is the concept of compounding. Put simply, it's the process of earning income on your original investment as well as on any income that has previously accumulated. It's effectively allowing your wealth to build itself, using your returns to earn even more returns.

Let's consider an example to illustrate the power of compounding. If you invest $10,000 with an annual return of 5%, after one year you would have $10,500. If you left the total amount in for another year and again achieved a 5% return, you would have $11,025. That extra $25 is the result of compound interest. Over the long term, the impact of compounding can be substantial.

5.4. Diversification

Diversification is one of the key tactics in managing investment risk. It implies spreading your investments across various assets classes (stocks, bonds, real estate, etc.), industries, or geographic locations with the intention of enhancing your potential returns and mitigating losses. Even if one investment performs poorly, others may perform well, effectively balancing out the overall investment performance.

In building a diversified portfolio, an investor should consider their risk tolerance, investment goals, and the time frame for which they are investing. Different asset classes and categories of investments have different risk-return profiles and behave differently over time.

5.5. Types of Investments

There are numerous types of investments that one can make, each carrying their own unique combination of risks and rewards. Here are some of the most common:

1. Stocks: When you buy stocks, also known as equities, you are buying a piece of a company. If the company does well, the price of the stock usually increases. Also, many companies pay regular dividends - a portion of the company's profits paid out to shareholders.

2. Bonds: Bonds, or fixed income securities, are essentially loans made by an investor to a borrower, typically corporate or governmental. The borrower promises to pay back the full amount loaned, plus interest.

3. Mutual Funds: A mutual fund is a type of managed portfolio. You put in money, and a professional fund manager buys a wide array of stocks, bonds, or other securities with it.

4. Real Estate: Real estate investments involve purchasing properties for rental income and/or the potential for profit from selling the property later.

5. ETFs: An Exchange Traded Fund (ETF) is a type of security that tracks an index, sector, commodity, or other asset, but can be

purchased or sold on a stock exchange the same way a regular stock can.

Investing is a crucial part of financial literacy and a significant contributor to personal wealth. It's a process by which individuals can make their money work for them, rather than just working for their money. Armed with an understanding of the fundamental concepts and principles, anyone can start to make educated decisions that will help them to secure their financial future.

Chapter 6. Decoding Debt and Managing Loans

As we step into the financial world, one of the first challenges we encounter is understanding the concept of debt and managing loans effectively. With societies becoming more credit-heavy, the ability to make well-informed decisions about taking and repaying loans is crucial for maintaining and enhancing financial health.

6.1. Understanding Debt

Before we proceed, it's vital to grasp what debt actually means. Fundamentally, debt is money owed by one party, the borrower, to another, the lender. This usually involves an agreement that the borrower will pay back the original amount plus interest over a designated period. Interest, often expressed as an annual percentage rate (APR), is essentially the cost of borrowing money from the lender. The amount of debt someone can manage depends on various factors, including income, living expenses, and other financial obligations.

6.2. Good Debt Vs. Bad Debt

Not all debt is created equal. Understanding the difference between "good debt" and "bad debt" can help you make better financial decisions.

"Good debt" is an investment that will grow in value or generate long-term income. Taking out student loans to pay for a college education can be considered good debt because it is an investment in your future earning power. Similarly, mortgage loans fall into this category, as they enable you to own an appreciating asset—your home.

On the other hand, "bad debt" involves borrowing for things that don't increase in value or generate income. An example of bad debt would be using a credit card to buy luxury items or vacations. If you can't pay off the balance at the end of the month, you're likely to incur high interest rates, making your purchases significantly more expensive than they originally were.

6.3. The Impact of Debt on Your Financial Health

Debt has a substantial impact on your overall financial health. It affects your credit score, a numerical rating that lenders use to evaluate your creditworthiness. The amount of debt you carry, especially compared to your total available credit (your credit utilization rate), is a significant factor in calculating your credit score.

High amounts of debt could lower your score, making it harder to secure loans in the future. Regular, on-time payments can help boost your credit score, while late payments can negatively affect it.

6.4. Dealing With Debt: Strategies and Tools

Once you understand the nature and impact of debt, it's time to take on strategies to deal with it.

1. **Budgeting**: Establishing a budget is a practical first step in taking control of your debt. Knowing where your money is going each month can show you where there's potential to save. This extra money can then be applied to reducing your debts.

2. **Debt Snowball Method**: For those with multiple debts, this strategy involves paying off debts in order from smallest to

largest balance. This approach allows for small wins up front, which can give a morale boost and make the process seem less daunting.

3. **Debt Avalanche Method**: Similar to the snowball strategy, this one tackles debts from highest to lowest interest rate. Over time, this method can save you more money in interest charges.

4. **Debt Consolidation**: If you have multiple loans, it might be beneficial to consolidate them into one loan with a potentially lower interest rate and simplified payment structure.

5. **Seeking Professional Advice**: You may also consider seeking help from a certified credit counselor or financial advisor, particularly if your debt situation feels overwhelming.

6.5. Managing Loans Efficiently

Besides managing the debts you have, it's also essential to gain proficiency in managing loans, which are structured forms of debts. Loans can come in many forms, each with different features, benefits, and drawbacks.

6.6. Types of Loans

1. **Secured Loans**: These loans are backed by an asset, such as a house in a mortgage loan or a car in an auto loan. The asset is seen as collateral that the lender can claim if you default on your loan.

2. **Unsecured Loans**: Unlike secured loans, these are not backed by collateral. Because they are riskier for lenders, they usually have higher interest rates. Personal loans and credit cards are examples of unsecured loans.

3. **Fixed-interest Loans**: The interest rate for these loans remains stable over the loan period, making it easier to budget for payments.

4. **Variable-interest Loans**: The interest rate for these loans changes based on market conditions. While you might get a lower rate initially, the rate could also rise significantly over time.

5. **Installment Loans**: These loans have a series of fixed payments spread out over a specified term. Student loans, auto loans, and mortgages are often installment loans.

6.7. Navigating Loan Agreements

Understanding your loan agreement is crucial before you sign on the dotted line. Pay attention to the APR, monthly payments, total repayment amount, late fees, and any penalties for repaying the loan early. Also, take note of the repayment schedule and ensure it aligns with your financial situation.

6.8. Conclusion

To be sure, financial literacy is a journey, not a sprint. It's important to approach it with patience and persistence. By demystifying debt and becoming proficient at managing loans, you'll equip yourself with essential skills to navigate the financial landscape and make informed decisions that promote your financial wellbeing. Take ownership of your financial future by learning, planning, and above all, asking when in doubt.

Chapter 7. Retirement Planning: Securing the Future

The inevitability of retirement is a crossroad that every working individual will come to face. Surviving and thriving during this anticipated phase of life requires suitable financial planning. This involves understanding retirement plans and devising effective income strategies that will facilitate a secure and comfortable retirement.

7.1. The Need for Retirement Planning

The proverb, "Failing to plan is planning to fail," holds particularly true when it comes to retirement. The goal of retirement planning is to ensure you have enough money to live on after ceasing paid work. With increased life expectancy, retirement can span decades, compounding the need for a well-funded retirement corpus. Notably, the risk of outliving one's savings is a terrifying prospect for many, and thus planning for retirement with due diligence is paramount.

Effective retirement planning enables: . Financial independence . Provision for healthcare costs . A cushion for unexpected expenses . Fulfillment of post-retirement dreams and goals

7.2. Understanding Retirement Risk Factors

Several risk factors can negatively impact your retirement savings. To manage these risks effectively, you must first identify and understand them.

Longevity Risk: Given the advancements in medical technology, life expectancy has significantly increased. Consequently, the risk of outliving your retirement savings is a genuine concern.

Inflation Risk: Inflation gradually erodes the value of your savings. The cost of living tends to increase over time, necessitating more funds to sustain the same lifestyle during retirement.

Investment Risk: Your savings are typically invested to fetch returns. However, investments come with a risk. Market volatility can cause the value of your investments to fluctitate, creating potential financial instability.

Healthcare Risk: With aging, healthcare needs and related costs can surge. These unexpected costs can deplete your retirement savings faster than anticipated.

7.3. Setting Retirement Goals

Retirement planning starts with defining your lifestyle goals for your retirement years. This could include living in a specific location, traveling, pursuing hobbies, or supporting causes you care about. Based on these goals, envision what annual income will be needed to support this lifestyle. Adjust this annual amount for inflation to get a rough estimate of your total retirement corpus.

7.4. Building Your Retirement Corpus

Once you have a target in mind, the next step involves exploring different channels to accumulate this corpus. The more diverse your portfolio, the more financially secure you can be.

Personal Savings: This is the most rudimentary form of building a retirement corpus. Regular saving, coupled with disciplined spending, adds up over time.

Employer-sponsored Retirement Plans: Most employers offer retirement benefits such as 401(k) or Simple IRA. Typically, a portion of your salary is directed towards these plans pre-tax, and often, employers match a part of your contribution.

Individual Retirement Accounts (IRAs): Traditional and Roth IRAs are excellent tools for saving retirement funds. While contributions to a traditional IRA may be tax-deductible, Roth IRA distributions are tax-free.

Health Savings Accounts (HSAs): For those who qualify, HSAs offer threefold tax benefits – deductions on contributions, tax-free earning, and withdrawals for qualifying healthcare costs are not taxed.

7.5. Ideal Investment Vehicles for Retirement

Investing wisely is key to growing your retirement corpus. Mutual funds, stocks, and bonds have been traditional favorites. More recently, exchange-traded funds (ETFs) and Real Estate Investment Trusts (REITs) have also proved popular. Strike a balance between risk and reward – younger investors can afford to assume more risks, while those nearing retirement should focus on capital preservation.

7.6. Creating a Retirement Budget

A retirement budget outlines your expected income and expenses during retirement. It's essential to factor in basic living expenses, healthcare, taxes, and discretionary spending. Review this periodically to accommodate changing circumstances.

7.7. Managing Retirement Funds

It's necessary to strike a balance between preserving your retirement corpus and generating a steady stream of income. Strategies like the 4% withdrawal rule, bucket approach, and the use of annuities can help ensure a steady income flow during retirement.

Retirement planning is an ongoing process that needs periodic review and adjustments. Stay updated on tax laws, market conditions and events that may impact your retirement plan. Remember that, while comprehensive retirement planning takes considerable time and effort, it's a crucial step towards ensuring a secure and fulfilling retirement.

In conclusion, building a financially secure retirement isn't a task to be procrastinated. Start today, consider seeking professional help if needed, and remember that successful retirement planning is a journey that culminates in the peace of mind and financial security that every retiree hopes to enjoy.

Chapter 8. The Role of Insurance in Financial Health

To ensure a comprehensive understanding, it is vital to first define what insurance is. In its essence, insurance refers to a financial product sold by insurance companies to safeguard the policyholder against the risk of a specified loss. It is a contract, commonly referred to as a policy, in which an individual or entity, for a financial consideration known as the premium, receives financial protection or reimbursement against losses.

8.1. The Nature of Risk

In finance, risk refers to the potential of losing financial resources or the uncertainty of a financial loss. Life is riddled with potentials for loss, from accidents and illnesses to burglaries and natural disasters. Life itself is precarious and insurance exists to mitigate this precariousness. Insurance caters for these uncertainties by distributing the risks from the insured to all the other people insured.

8.2. Types of Insurance

There is a wide range of insurance products available, each designed to protect against different types of potential losses. The most common types are life insurance, health insurance, auto insurance, property insurance, and liability insurance.

Life Insurance offers financial benefits to a decedent's family or other designated beneficiaries and may specifically provide for income to an insured person's family, burial, funeral, and other final expenses.

Health Insurance covers medical expenses, from routine check-ups to emergency surgeries. It can also cover prescriptions and hospital stays.

Auto Insurance protects the policyholder against financial loss in the event of an incident involving a vehicle they own.

Property Insurance protects the owner or renter of a structure and its contents from damage caused by fires, storms, and other risks.

Liability Insurance provides the insured party with protection against claims resulting from injuries and damage to people and/or property.

8.3. Why Insurance is Crucial for Financial Health

Insurance serves several essential functions in a financial plan.

1. **Risk Management**: Insurance assists individuals in managing risk and the potential financial fallout from unexpected events. By obtaining insurance, policyholders can pay a known premium for protection against significant uncertain losses.

2. **Peace of Mind**: By purchasing insurance, individuals gain peace of mind knowing they have a financial buffer for unwelcome surprises. This security contributes to overall mental well-being, improving quality of life.

3. **Financial Stability**: Insurance payouts offer financial help when it's needed most. For example, life insurance could prevent a bereaved family from financial hardship, while health insurance could guard against bankruptcy due to medical bills.

4. **Protect Assets**: Auto and homeowners insurance are concretely about preserving the assets you've worked hard to acquire. A car accident or home disaster could be financially devastating

without insurance.

5. **Manage Cash Flow**: Insurance provides a means to manage cash flow uncertainty. Insurance provides payment for covered losses when they occur. Therefore, the uncertainty of paying for the losses out-of-pocket is reduced significantly.

8.4. Understanding Insurance Policies

An insurance policy is a contract between the insured and the insurance company. It outlines what the insurance company will cover and under what circumstances they will pay out a claim. Therefore, it's important that policyholders thoroughly understand what their policy covers.

1. **Premium**: This is the amount of money an individual or business pays for an insurance policy.

2. **Policy Limit**: This is the maximum amount an insurance company will pay under a policy for a covered loss.

3. **Deductible**: This is the amount you pay out of pocket for expenses before the insurance company will cover the remaining costs.

4. **Claim**: This is a formal request by a policyholder to an insurance company for coverage or compensation for a covered loss or policy event.

8.5. In Conclusion

Insurance isn't just about paying monthly premiums - it's about having a safety net, providing you with financial security when you need it most. Insurance is a tool that lessens financial risks and brings peace of mind, stability, and integrity into our lives – a vital cornerstone for anyone's financial health. Understanding the role of insurance, types of insurance, and the terminology will aid you in making confident decisions that support your financial wellness.

Remember, the most expensive insurance policy is the one you need but didn't buy. Make sure to assess your financial situation, understand your needs, and select the right insurance policies. Insurance is more than just a purchase; it's an investment in your financial health. This solid foundation of understanding and proper utilization of insurance will lead you towards ultimate financial stability and security.

Chapter 9. Mortgages, Real Estate and Their Influence

In the realm of personal finance, understanding mortgages and real estate, and their influence on one's financial health, is of paramount importance. The complex variables that these entities bring with them are often responsible for shaping an individual's long-term financial progress and stability.

9.1. The Dynamics of Mortgages

Owning a home is a common aspiration shared by many, making mortgages widely appealing. A mortgage is essentially a long term loan taken out by individuals or businesses to finance the purchase of a property, secured by that property until it's fully paid off. Simply put, a mortgage is used by potential home buyers to raise money to buy real estate or by existing homeowners to raise funds for any purpose while putting a lien on the owned property.

Even though the borrower is the legal property owner, the lender holds an interest in the property while payments are being made. This means that the lender, most often a financial institution such as a bank, could take possession of the property if the borrower fails to meet the repayment terms of the mortgage.

Obtaining a mortgage enables individuals to buy a home without having to pay the entire cost upfront. Instead, the borrower repays the loan, plus interest, over a set period, usually between 15 and 30 years.

9.2. Understanding Your Mortgage

When determining your ability to pay back a mortgage loan, lenders consider your credit score, current income, and job history. The loan terms vary depending on factors but ideally consist of four parts:

1. Loan amount: This is the total amount that you borrow from a lender.

2. Interest rate: This is the percentage of the loan amount that the lender charges to borrow money.

3. Loan term: This is the length of time that you have to repay the money to the lender. The most common loan terms are 15 and 30 years.

4. Payment: This is the amount you pay each month to reduce both your principal balance and the interest accrued.

9.3. The Benefits of Mortgages

A mortgage comes with a number of benefits that makes it a popular choice:

1. Home Ownership: It enables people to become homeowners without needing large amounts of cash upfront.

2. Fixed Costs: If you opt for a fixed-rate mortgage, the interest rate stays the same for the term of the loan, helping budgeting as your mortgage payment won't change drastically over the life of your loan.

3. Property Appreciation: Over the long run, real estate has generally appreciated in value, so a home purchased via a mortgage could increase in value over time.

4. Tax Benefits: The interest paid on a mortgage is tax-deductible, reducing the amount of tax you'll owe each year.

9.4. The Flip Side: The Risks of Mortgages

While mortgages provide the opportunity to buy a home, they come with significant responsibility and potential financial risk. Failure to repay the mortgage loan can result in foreclosure, in which the lender takes control of the property. High-interest rates, job loss, or other financial hardships can make it difficult to keep up with mortgage payments, potentially leading to this unfortunate outcome.

Moreover, property value is not guaranteed to increase. If it decreases, you could find yourself with a mortgage loan that is higher than the value of your home.

9.5. Real Estate: The investment potential and its influence

Real estate, whether we're speaking of residential, commercial, or rental properties, has been a stand-by for investors, both individual and institutional. It provides a tangible way to diversify an investment portfolio and potentially increase net worth over time, unlike other asset classes.

An investment in real estate could provide income streams and significant profit potential. Rental properties, for example, can provide a steady income stream while the property potentially appreciates in value. The same applies to commercial real estate — businesses pay rent to use the investor's property.

Real estate values also have the potential to rise over time, offering investors the chance for significant capital gains. One aspect that uniquely separates real estate from other asset classes is leverage. With leverage, a small amount of money can control a large valuable asset that has the potential to appreciate over time.

9.6. Risks of Real Estate Investing

As valuable as real estate can be as an asset class, it doesn't come without risks. These assets are relatively illiquid compared to stocks and bonds. This means they cannot be bought and sold as quickly, and their prices can often be negotiable.

Market risk is by far the most significant risk associated with real estate. The possibility that the real estate market will be in a downturn when you need to sell is a serious concern.

Moreover, managing properties is not easy and requires significant time, money, and expertise to be done correctly. Negative occurrences such as the absence of tenants, slight downturns in the neighborhood, or major repairs can turn a good investment into a poor one.

To conclude, mortgages and real estate play a vital role in an individual's overall financial health. While they offer significant benefits and potential for assurance in financial independence and security, they require a close understanding of the housing market, careful planning, and sound financial judgement to navigate effectively. However, if approached wisely and with suitable advice, these can be instrumental in building wealth.

Chapter 10. Taxes: The Necessary Obligation and How to Navigate Them

Taxes are a fundamental part of any society. These compulsory financial obligations we owe to the government are crucial in funding necessary public services and infrastructure. It's essential to understand how they affect your income and investments, and learning how to navigate the complex world of taxes can prove incredibly useful, potentially saving you a substantial amount of money. Here, we will break down everything you need to know about taxes - from tax brackets to deductions, credits, and ways to optimize your tax liability.

10.1. Understanding Taxes: The Basics

Taxes come in several forms, including income tax, sales tax, property tax, corporate tax, capital gains tax, and more. However, our primary focus is on personal income tax - a tax levied on individuals or entities depending on their income or profits.

In the United States, a progressive tax system is used for income tax meaning tax rates increase as the taxable amount increases. The federal government categorizes income ranges into tax brackets. Each tax bracket has a different rate, which applies to the income that falls within that bracket.

Income tax can also come in the form of withholding tax, where your employer deducts a portion of your income to directly pay it to the government. This is typically seen in W-2 wage and tax statements.

10.2. Deductions and Credits: Lowering Your Tax Liability

Deductions and credits are two key features of the tax code that can lower your overall tax bill. It's important to understand the difference between the two and how they impact your taxable income.

1. Tax Deductions: These reduce your taxable income, meaning they decrease the amount of your income that is subject to tax. Deductions come in different forms - the standard deduction, itemized deductions, and above-the-line deductions.

   a. Standard Deduction: This is a flat amount that the tax code allows you to deduct from your income each year. The amount depends on your filing status.

   b. Itemized Deductions: These include specific expenses allowed by the tax code that you can deduct from your income. They include medical expenses, state and local taxes, mortgage interest, and charitable donations.

   c. Above-the-Line Deductions: These are deductions that any taxpayer can take. They are subtracted directly from your gross income and include student loan interest, teaching supplies, and more.

2. Tax Credits: These are amounts that are subtracted directly from the taxes you owe, unlike deductions which reduce taxable income. Credits can be refundable (they can reduce your tax liability beyond zero, and offer a refund) or non-refundable (they can only reduce tax liability to zero).

10.3. Strategies for Tax Efficiency

1. Retirement Contributions: Maximizing contributions to your retirement accounts not only prepares you for the future but also

offers tax benefits. Traditional IRA and 401(k) contributions reduce your taxable income in the year you make them.

2. Tax-Loss Harvesting: This technique allows you to use the losses from one investment to offset the gains from another, thereby reducing your capital gains tax.

3. Charitable Contributions: Donations to qualified charitable organizations can be deducted from your income, reducing your overall tax liability.

10.4. Dealing with Tax Debts

If you find yourself owing more than you can pay in taxes, don't panic. The IRS provides several options to help taxpayers who owe taxes, penalties, or interest, including installment agreements, offer in compromise, and temporary delay of the collection process.

10.5. The Importance of Tax Planning

Tax planning is a comprehensive analysis of a taxpayer's financial situation from a tax perspective. It ensures tax efficiency, considering all the elements of a financial plan that can affect your tax liability. A good tax plan can help maximize savings and investments while minimizing the tax liability.

Remember, everyone's tax situation is different. It's crucial to consult with an expert or use reliable tax software to ensure you meet your tax obligations correctly and take advantage of any potential savings. The more you understand about taxes, the easier you'll find to navigate this necessary obligation.

Chapter 11. Planning for Major Life Events

Planning for major life events embodies the essence of financial literacy. It is the process wherein you ensure that you have the necessary financial resources to successfully navigate significant occurrences in your life, such as getting an education, buying a home, marriage, starting a family, and retirement planning. The steps involved include setting specific, measurable, achievable, relevant, and time-bound (SMART) goals, analyzing the financial requirements, creating a financial plan, and continually reviewing and making adjustments to the plan as required.

11.1. Identifying Major Life Events

Before laying out plans for major life events, you must first recognize what these events will likely be in your own life. Everyone's journey is different, so your important life events may differ from those of your peers or family. However, some significant hallmarks may be uniform across many lives. These can include leaving home, furthering your education, starting a career, getting married, buying a house, starting a family, and retirement.

Establish SMART goals associated with these milestones. Decide on what you want to accomplish, define it precisely, ensure it is an achievable goal, confirm it aligns with your other life objectives, and set a timeframe for when you want to reach it.

11.2. Estimating Financial Requirements

Once you've mapped your major life events, your next step is to determine the financial resources you would need to make them happen. This requires first understanding the costs associated with each event and then taking into account your current resources and projected income.

It's important to consider short-term and long-term expenses. For instance, while planning for a house, consider upfront costs like down payment, moving expenses, and furniture as well as ongoing costs such as mortgage payments, property taxes, home insurance, and maintenance.

Moreover, keep in mind that costs can often rise over time due to inflation. Hence, you should factor this into your estimations.

11.3. Creating a Financial Plan

Now that you have a clear idea about what financial resources you'd need, it's time to create a plan about how you can save for them. Your plan should specify the steps you'll take to save and grow your wealth.

First, determine your saving capacity by deducting your expenses from your income. Look for opportunities to increase your income or reduce your expenses to maximize your savings.

Next, identify the right savings or investment vehicles that match your risk tolerance and the timeframe for your goal. For short term goals, you might favor a high-yield savings account or certificate of deposit. For long-term goals, investing in the stock market or real estate might be more appropriate given they often yield a higher return over the long run.

Consider using automated payments or transfers to a designated account to ensure consistent saving.

Creating a plan also involves figuring out how to tackle any existing debt that could hamper your saving ability.

11.4. Reviewing and Adjusting the Plan

A financial plan isn't a set-it-and-forget-it affair. As you progress through life, circumstances may change, requiring you to revisit and revise your plan. A new job, the birth of a child, or unexpected expenses can all call for adjustments.

Review your plan regularly - at least once a year. Take note of any new financial goals and incorporate them into your existing plan. If you experienced any financial windfalls, like bonuses or inheritances, decide on how to allocate them across your goals.

This regular review also lets you monitor your investments and ensure they are performing as expected. If they are not, you should consider finding more suitable alternatives.

11.5. Dealing with Uncertain Events

Life can be unpredictable, and you should build some flexibility into your plans to ensure your financial security does not falter due to unexpected events.

Creating an emergency fund can provide peace of mind and a robust financial safety net. Make sure it's enough to cover at least three to six months' worth of living expenses.

Consider insurance, from health to auto to home, to shield yourself from significant losses. Especially as you age, life insurance and long-term care insurance can protect you and your loved ones.

Planning for major life events is a critical facet of being financially literate. By understanding your financial needs, setting SMART goals, and reviewing your plan regularly, you can ensure you're prepared for the milestones in your life journey. Remember that the journey is often as important as the destination, and thorough planning will ensure the journey is smoother and more enjoyable.

www.ingramcontent.com/pod-product-compliance
Lightning Source LLC
Chambersburg PA
CBHW071044260726
48661CB00007B/3143